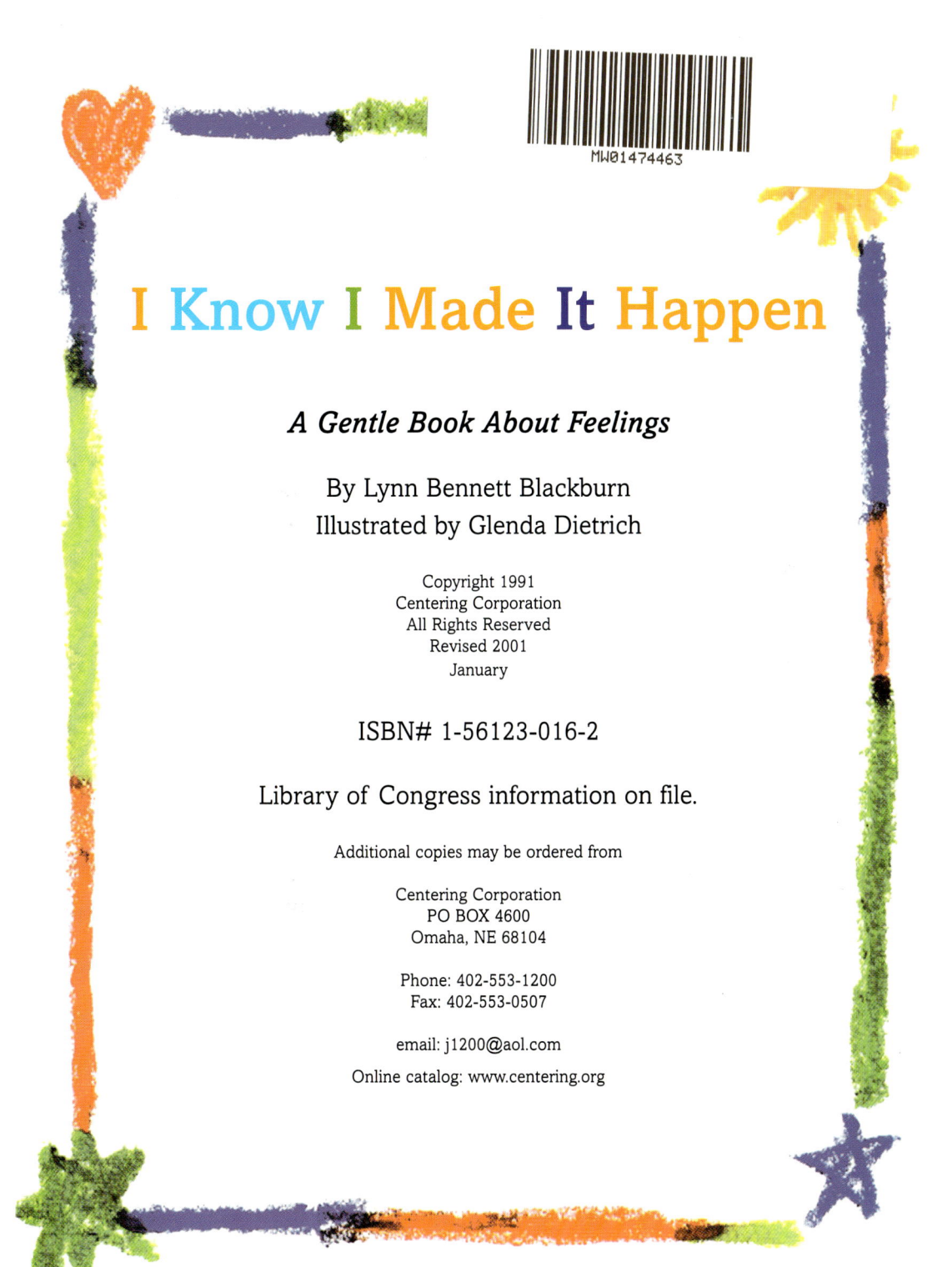

I Know I Made It Happen

A Gentle Book About Feelings

By Lynn Bennett Blackburn
Illustrated by Glenda Dietrich

Copyright 1991
Centering Corporation
All Rights Reserved
Revised 2001
January

ISBN# 1-56123-016-2

Library of Congress information on file.

Additional copies may be ordered from

Centering Corporation
PO BOX 4600
Omaha, NE 68104

Phone: 402-553-1200
Fax: 402-553-0507

email: j1200@aol.com

Online catalog: www.centering.org

Today my sister fell out of a tree.
She scraped her arm and bumped her head.
She cried for a long time.

I know I made it happen.

I was mad because she wouldn't let me climb first.
I told her I hoped she'd break a leg.
She told me to shut up.
Then her hand slipped.
She fell.

I know I made it happen.
Grandma says words can't make my sister fall.
Her hand slipped and that made her fall.
Grandma said, "Remember how you slipped on the stairs?
Your foot got caught. That made you fall."

She says accidents just happen.

I still felt sad inside.
I couldn't make that feeling go away.

Grandma suggested we play a game with my sister.
She said I would see that my words didn't make her fall.

She said I can do things to help me feel better.

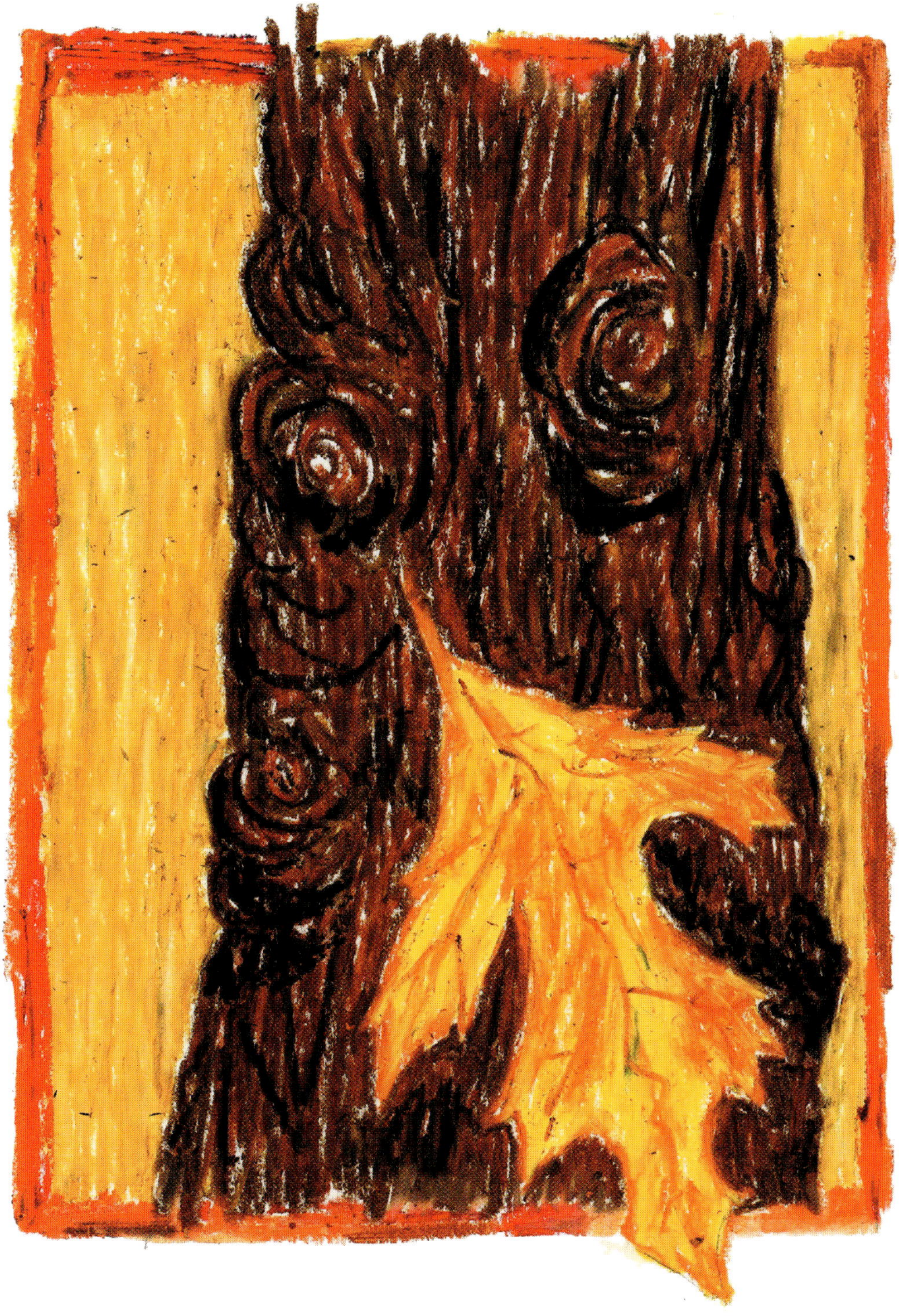

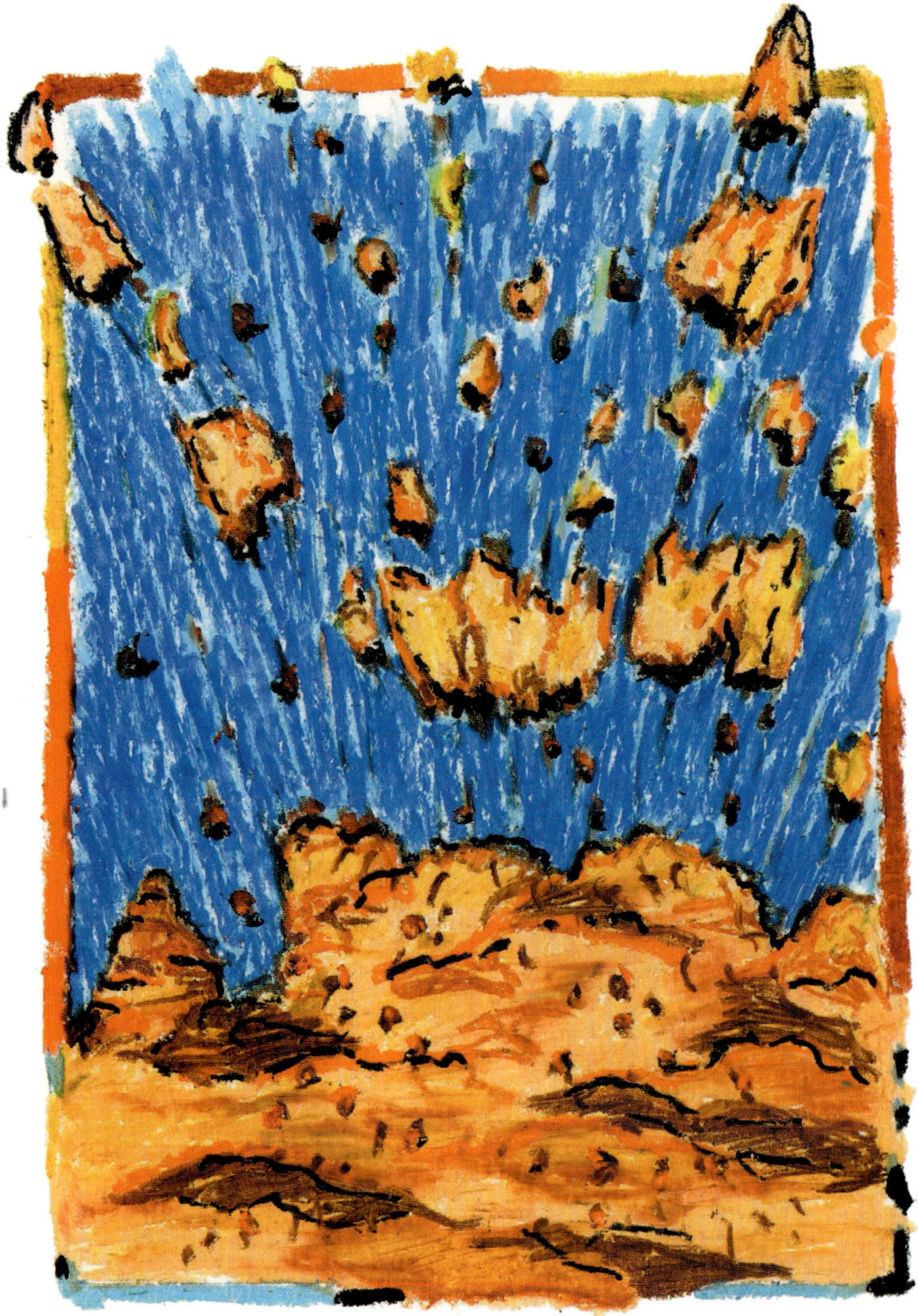

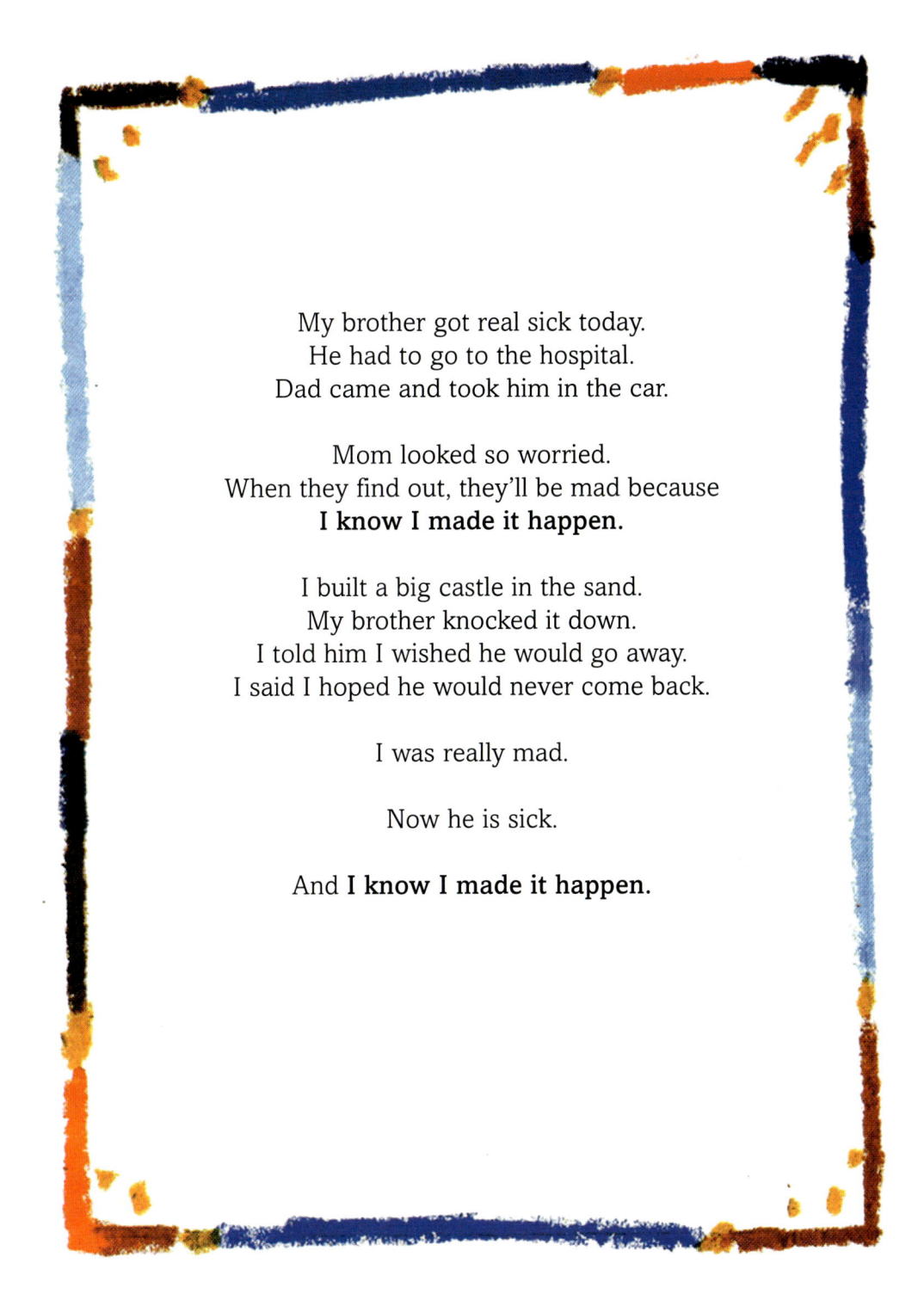

My brother got real sick today.
He had to go to the hospital.
Dad came and took him in the car.

Mom looked so worried.
When they find out, they'll be mad because
I know I made it happen.

I built a big castle in the sand.
My brother knocked it down.
I told him I wished he would go away.
I said I hoped he would never come back.

I was really mad.

Now he is sick.

And **I know I made it happen.**

I'm scared and worried, too.

Mom could see I was scared.
She let me talk to the nurse who was taking care of my brother.
The nurse said germs made my brother sick.
She said he'd be home soon.
She said no one knows just why he got sick.

Getting sick just happens.

I felt so left out.
I wanted to help.
Finally, I figured out what to do.

I took some paper and crayons and made a lot of good pictures.
I decorated his room with the pictures.
Decorations don't make germs go away,
but his smile when he saw them helped me feel better.

We played a game together on his bed.
We laughed and had fun.

I told him I was sorry I'd been mad at him.
He looked at me and smiled.
He didn't even remember how I'd yelled at him.

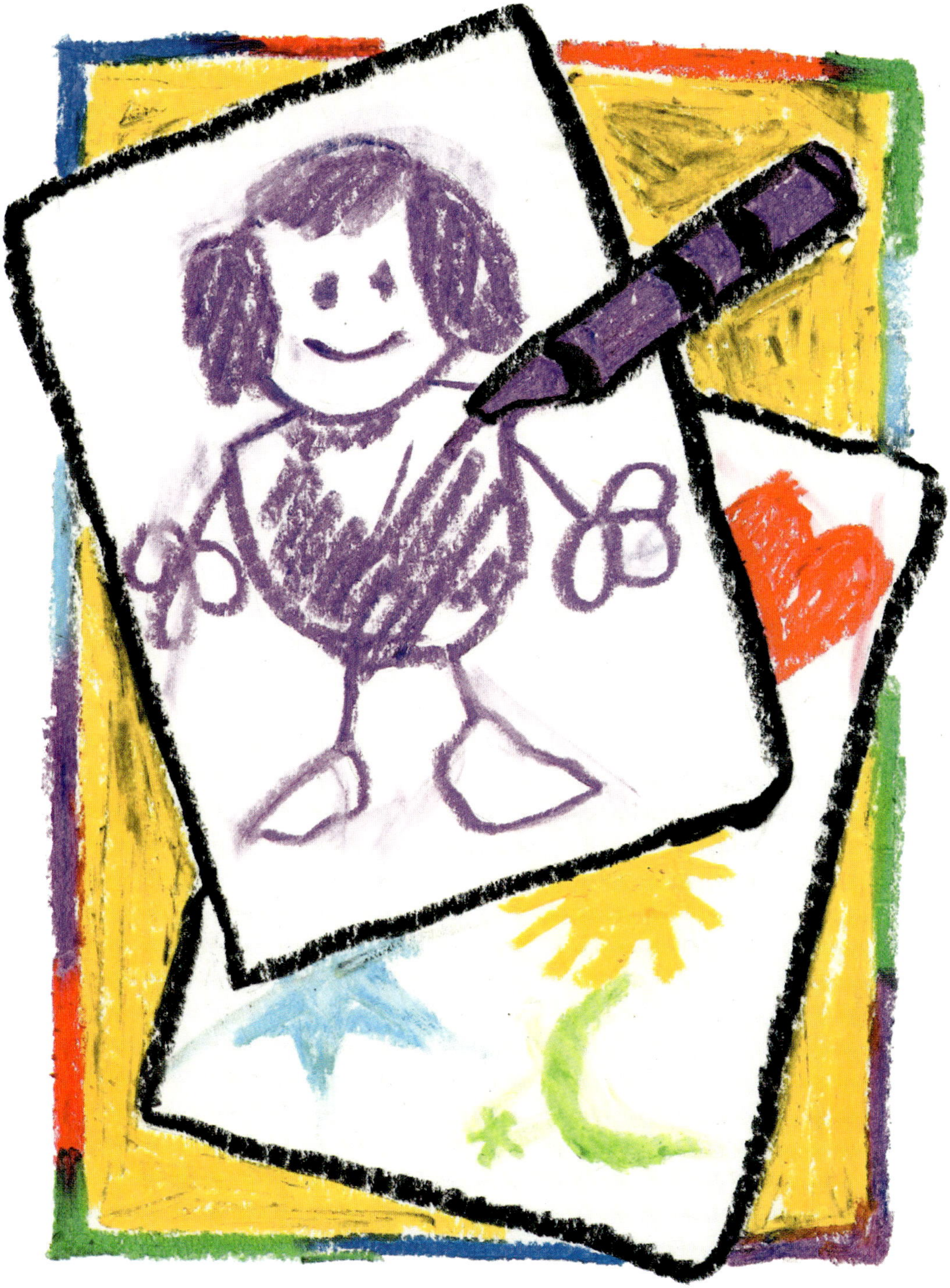

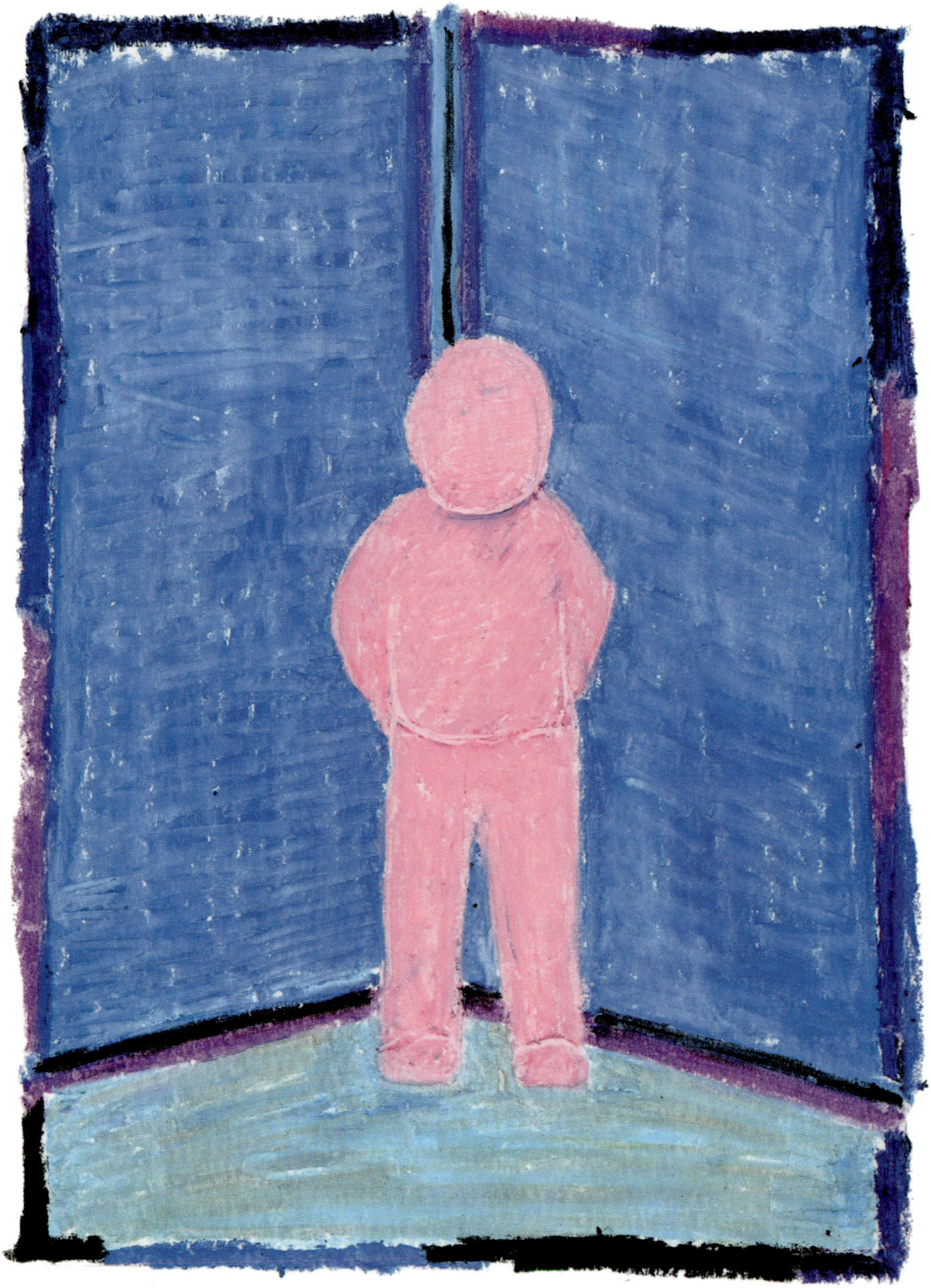

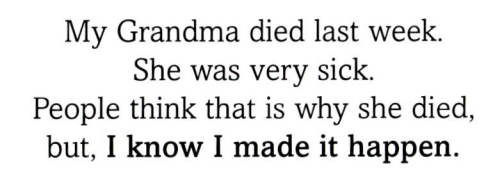

My Grandma died last week.
She was very sick.
People think that is why she died,
but, **I know I made it happen.**

It scared me to think about her dying.
So, I wished that if she had to die,
she'd do it soon.
She did.

And **I know I made it happen.**

I was scared to go into her room.
When my Mom went to visit her, I stayed in a corner.

She smiled and talked to me for a little while.
I smiled back, but I was scared.

Maybe if I had been a better visitor
she would be alive today.

I told my teacher I made her die.
He reminded me about the fight I had with Eddie last week
and how I told him I wished he would drop dead.

He didn't.

Wishes must not work.

Death happens when a person is too old
or too sick to live.

Nothing I thought or did or wished
made my Grandma die.

But I was so scared and so angry,
I never said goodbye to my Grandma.

Now she is dead.

I felt bad inside for not saying goodbye.

I never got to tell her I loved her.

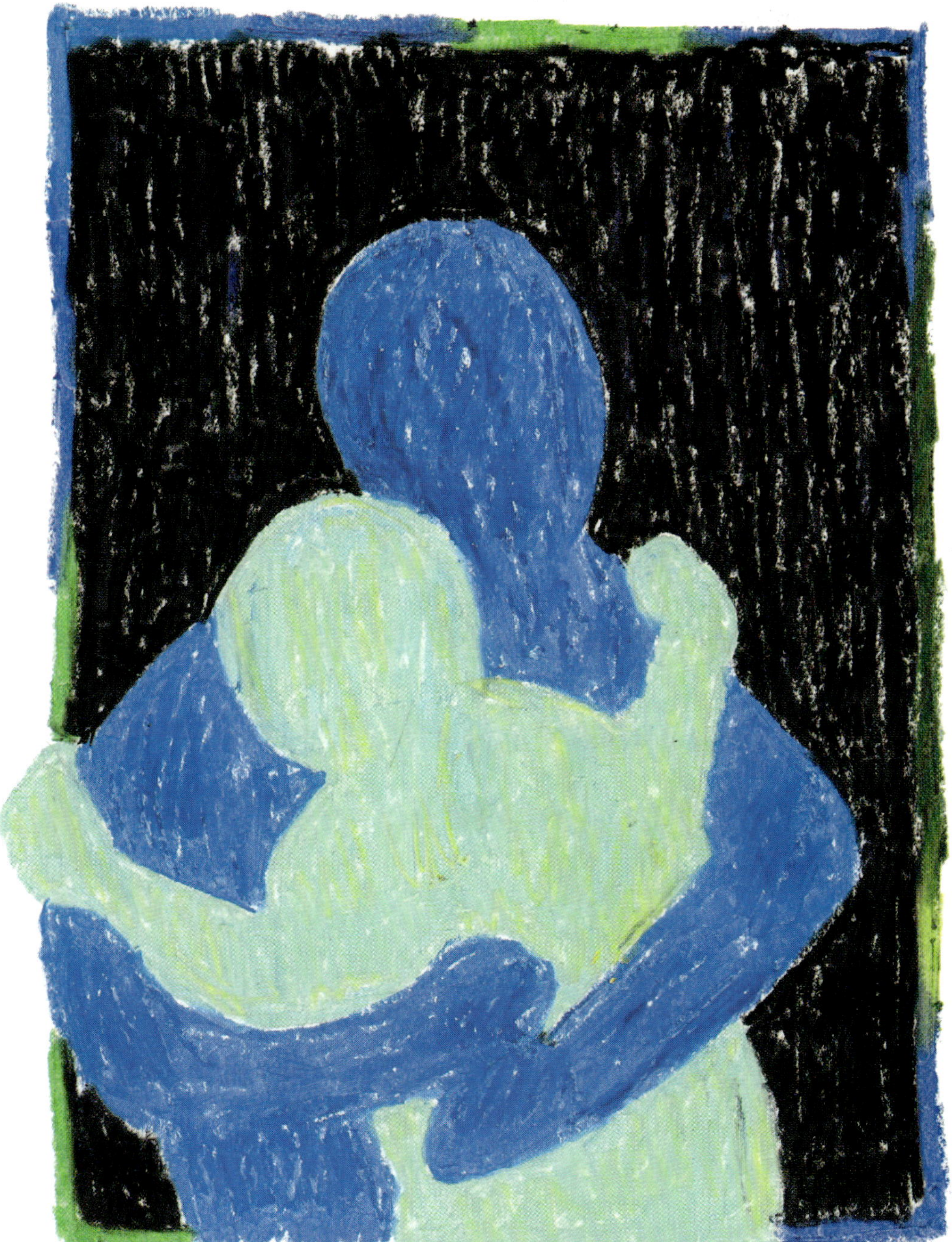

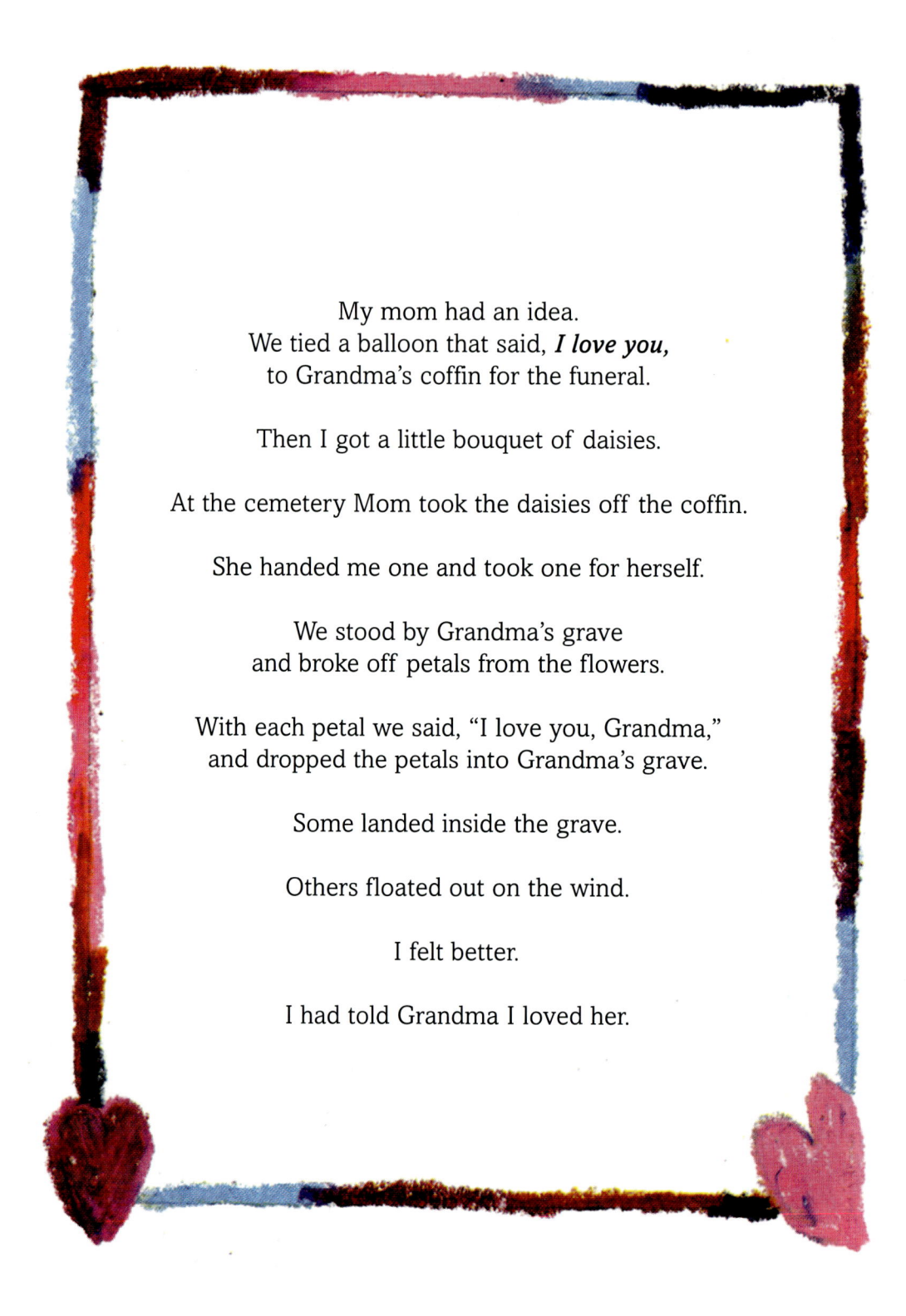

My mom had an idea.
We tied a balloon that said, *I love you,*
to Grandma's coffin for the funeral.

Then I got a little bouquet of daisies.

At the cemetery Mom took the daisies off the coffin.

She handed me one and took one for herself.

We stood by Grandma's grave
and broke off petals from the flowers.

With each petal we said, "I love you, Grandma,"
and dropped the petals into Grandma's grave.

Some landed inside the grave.

Others floated out on the wind.

I felt better.

I had told Grandma I loved her.

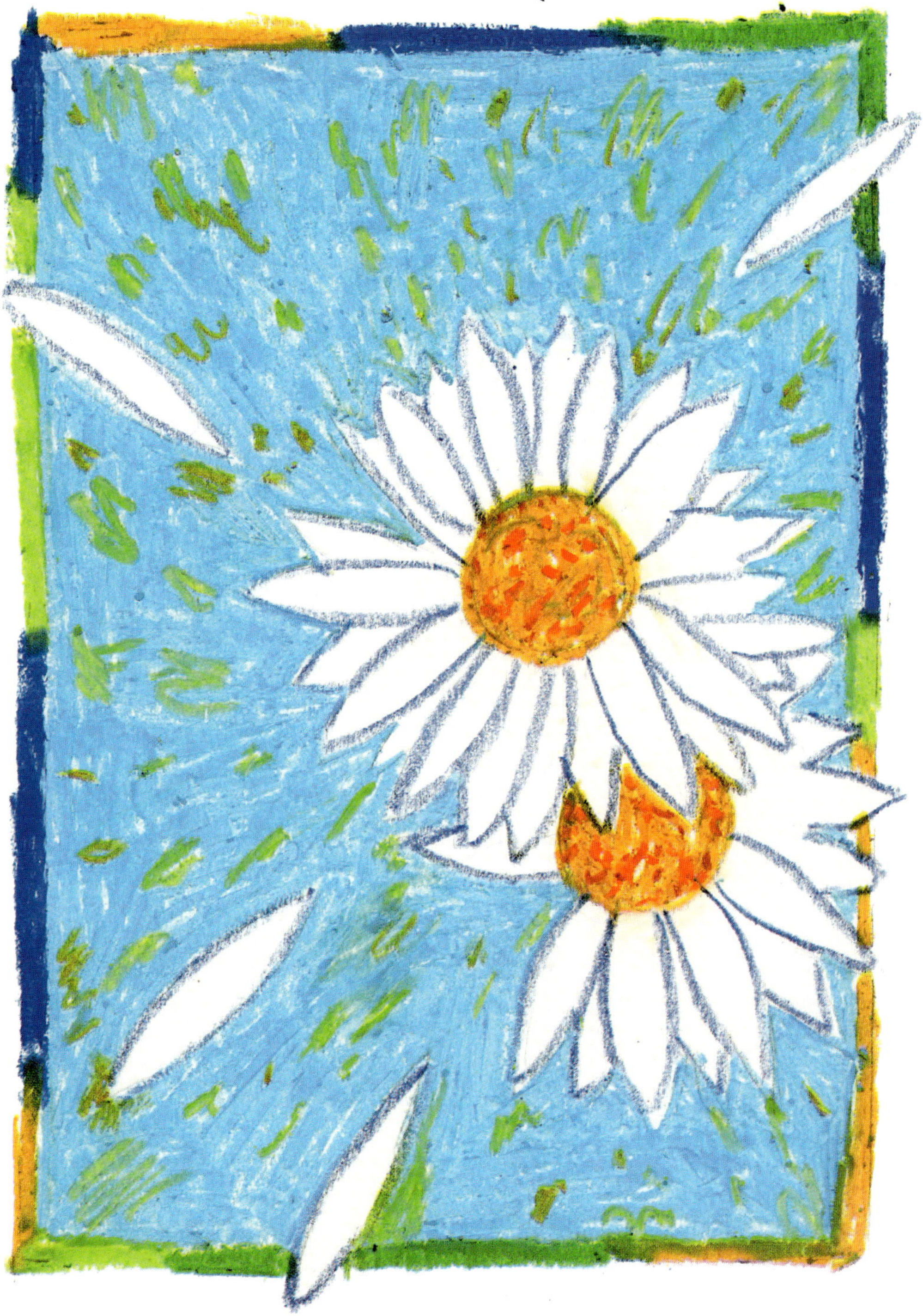

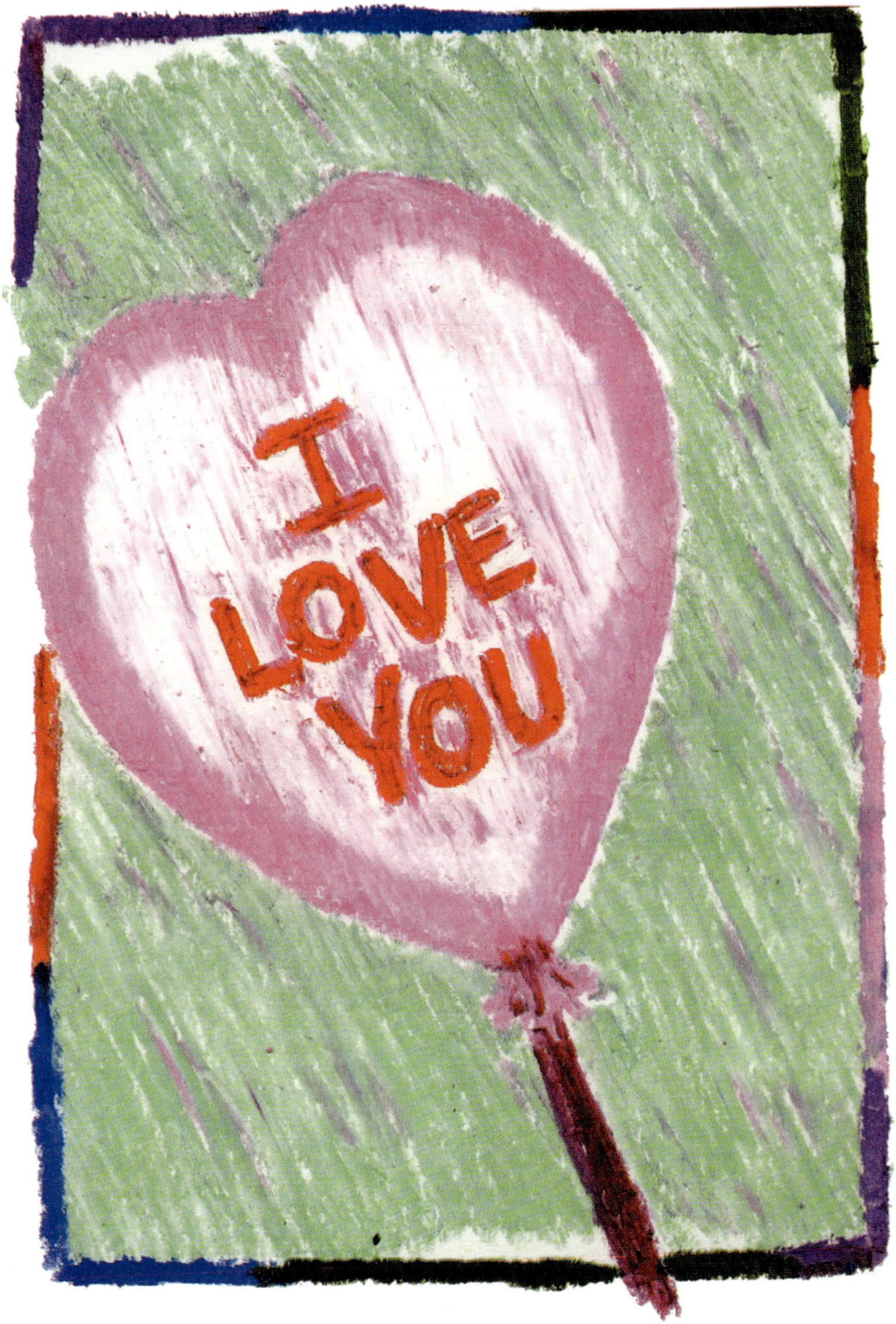
I LOVE YOU

Mom untied the balloon, too.

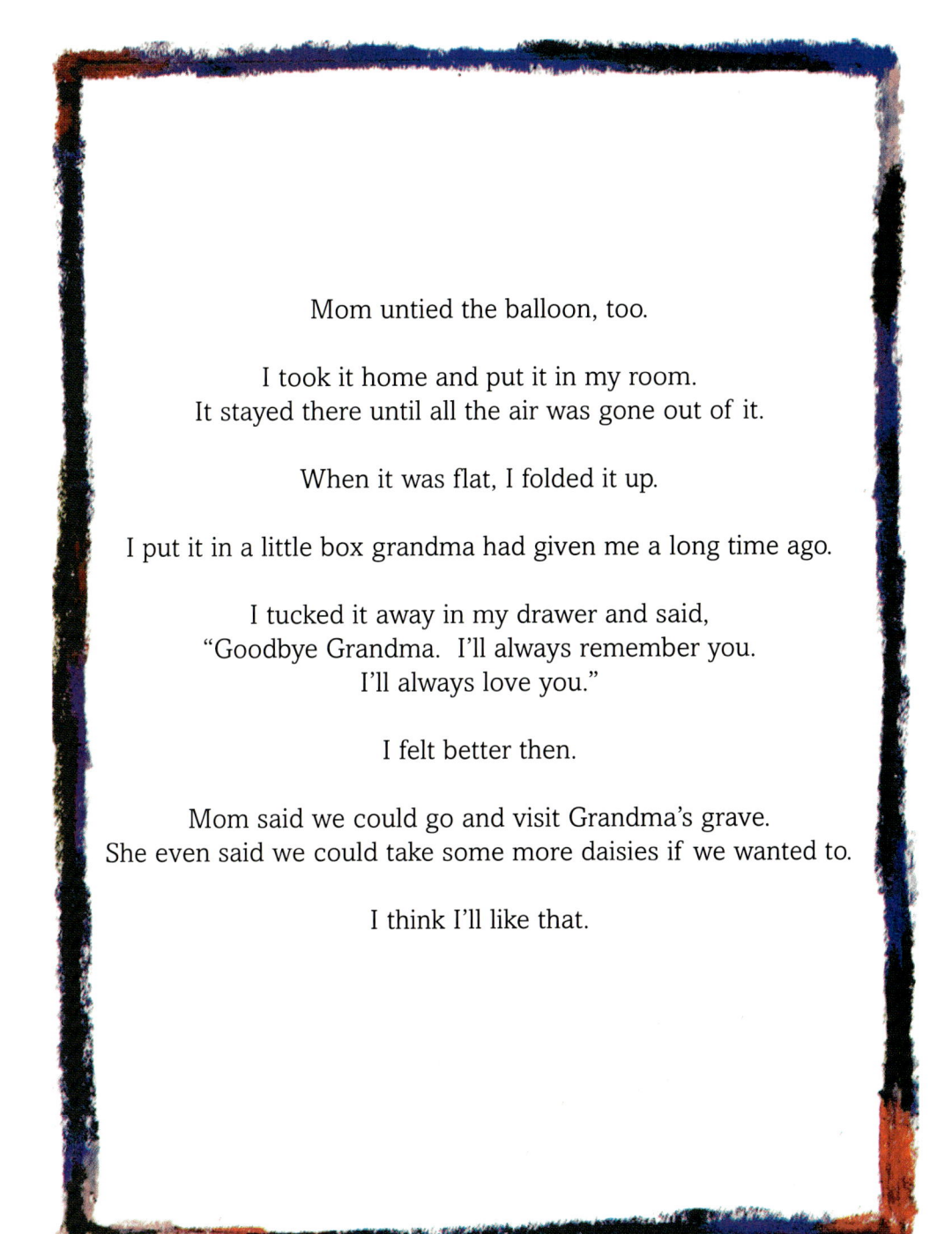

I took it home and put it in my room.
It stayed there until all the air was gone out of it.

When it was flat, I folded it up.

I put it in a little box grandma had given me a long time ago.

I tucked it away in my drawer and said,
"Goodbye Grandma. I'll always remember you.
I'll always love you."

I felt better then.

Mom said we could go and visit Grandma's grave.
She even said we could take some more daisies if we wanted to.

I think I'll like that.

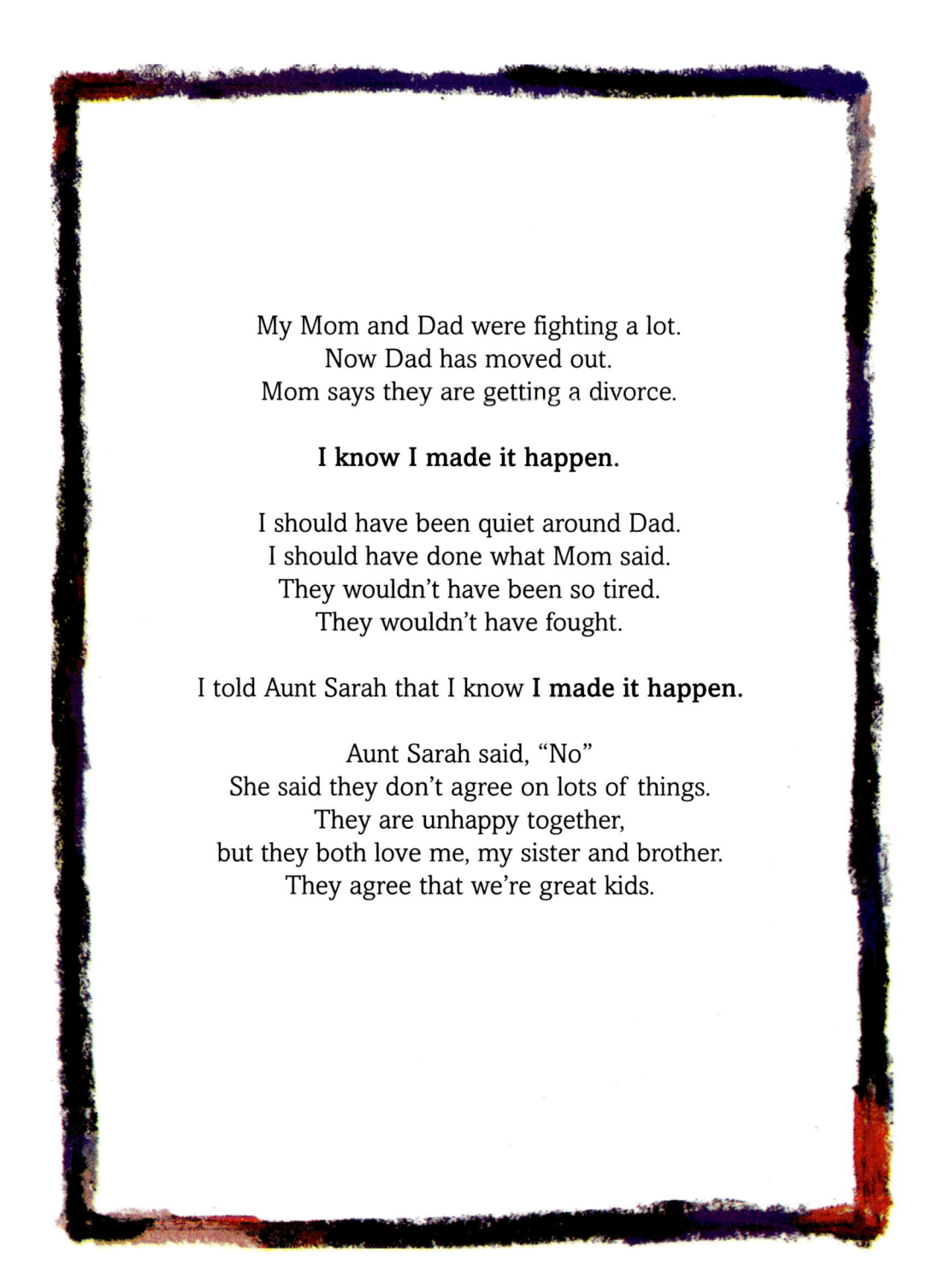

My Mom and Dad were fighting a lot.
Now Dad has moved out.
Mom says they are getting a divorce.

I know I made it happen.

I should have been quiet around Dad.
I should have done what Mom said.
They wouldn't have been so tired.
They wouldn't have fought.

I told Aunt Sarah that I know **I made it happen.**

Aunt Sarah said, "No"
She said they don't agree on lots of things.
They are unhappy together,
but they both love me, my sister and brother.
They agree that we're great kids.

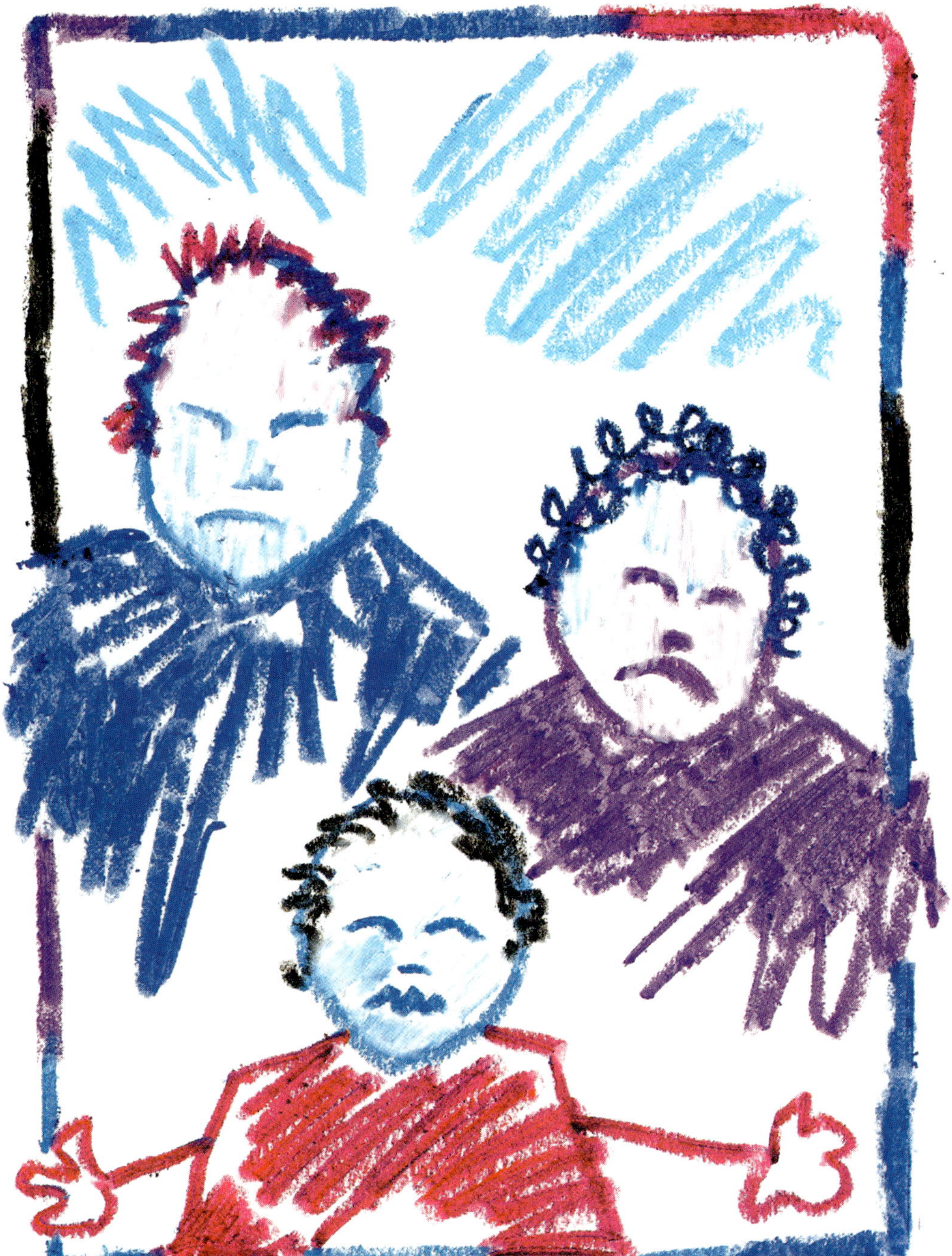

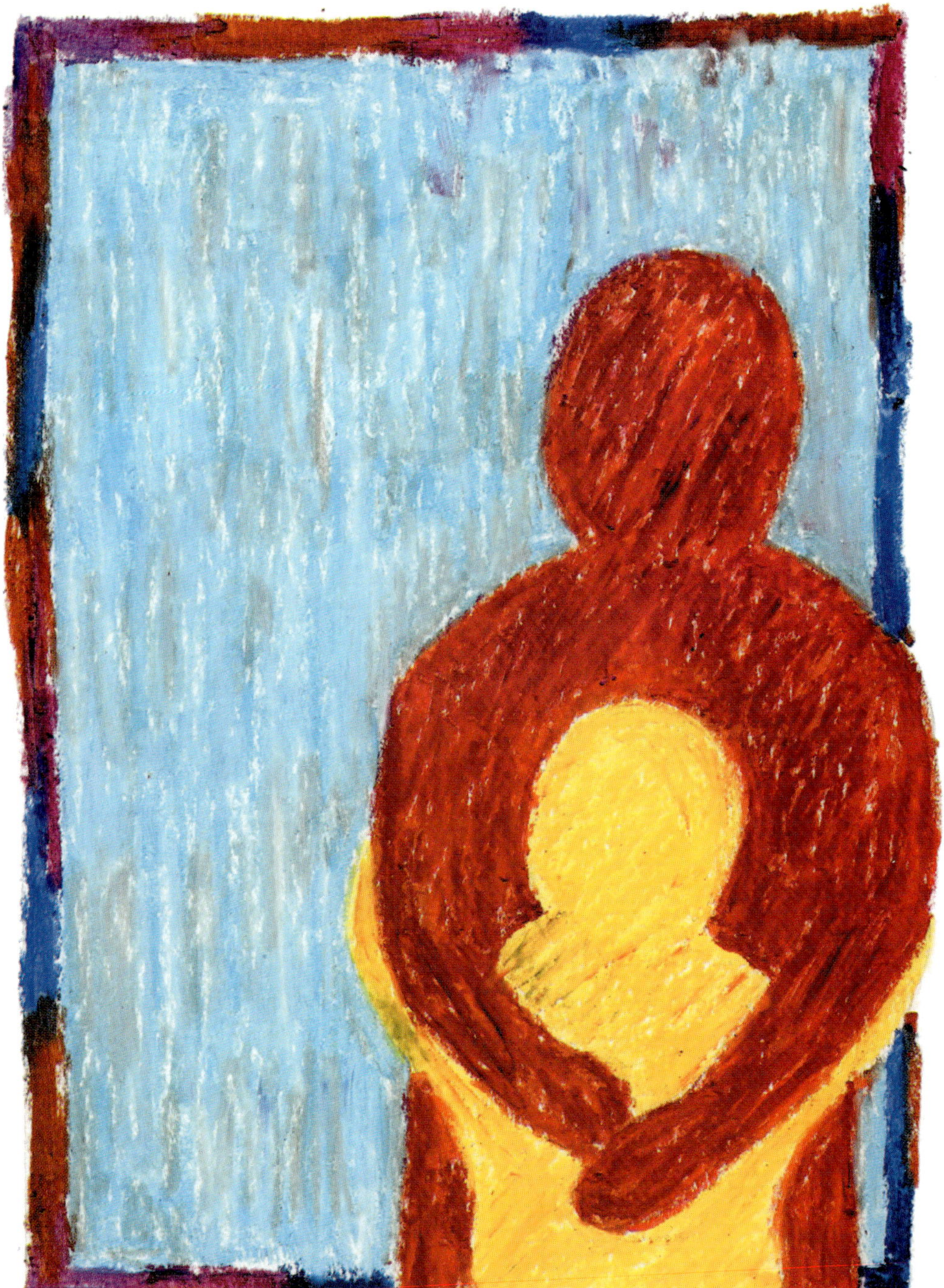

She said feelings and people change.

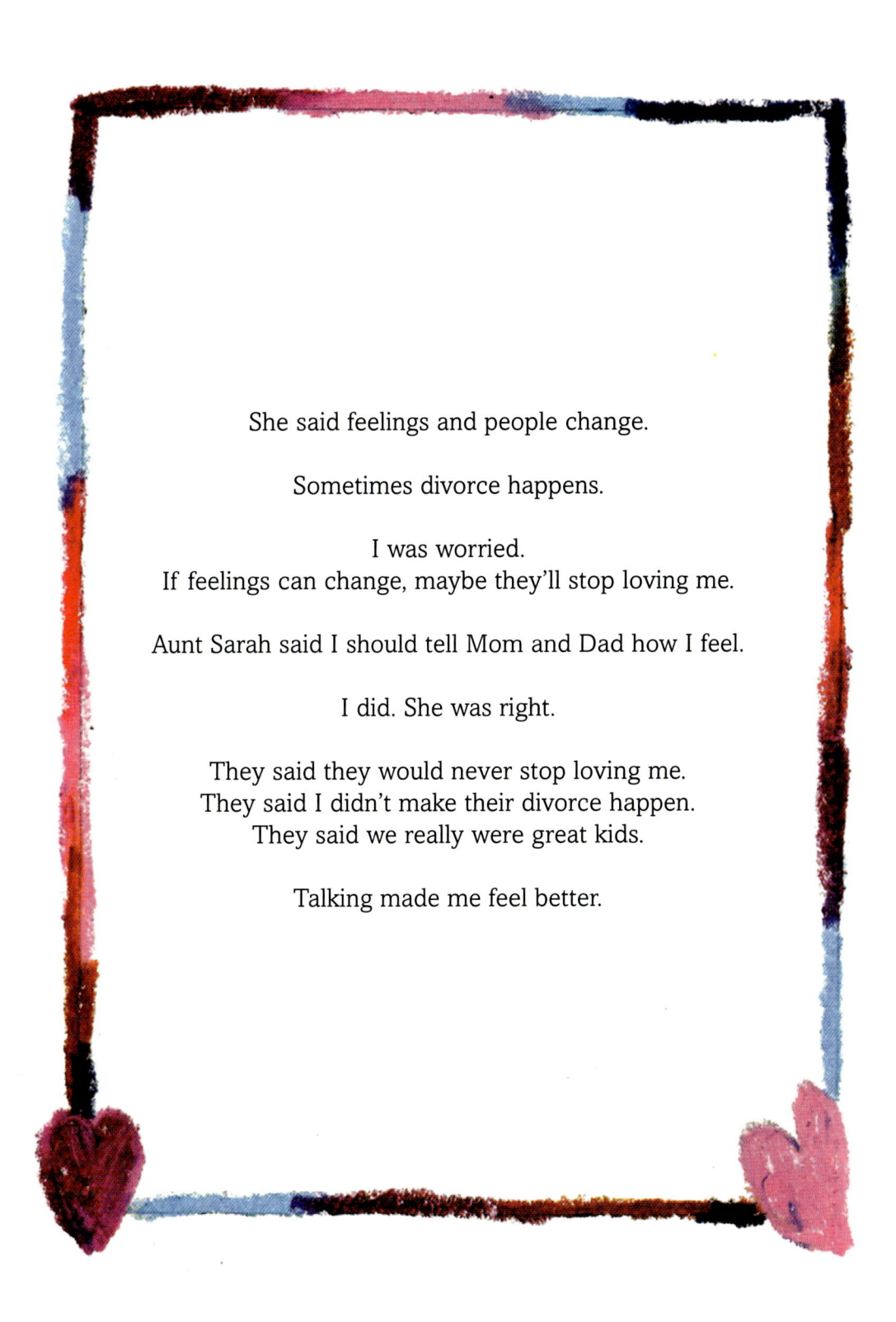

Sometimes divorce happens.

I was worried.
If feelings can change, maybe they'll stop loving me.

Aunt Sarah said I should tell Mom and Dad how I feel.

I did. She was right.

They said they would never stop loving me.
They said I didn't make their divorce happen.
They said we really were great kids.

Talking made me feel better.

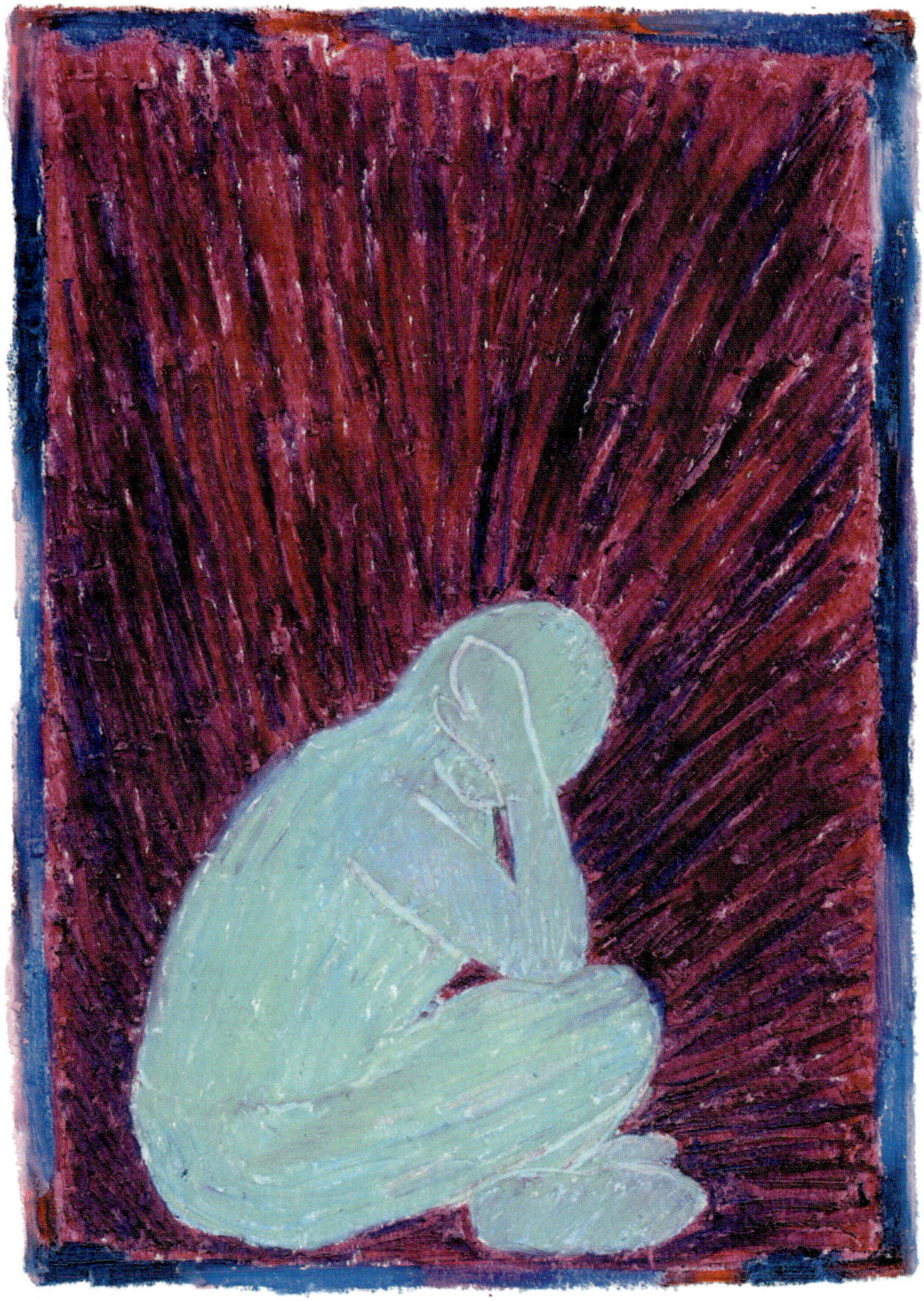

It's hard to understand that people have accidents.
It's hard to understand how people get old or sick and die.
It's hard to understand that sometimes people get a divorce.

There are a lot of things that are hard to understand.

If there was someone to blame,
someone who really made all of these things happen,
maybe I could understand better.

If I knew there was a reason,
that would help, too.

But a lot of times, no one is to blame.
There doesn't seem to be any reason at all.

It's nice to know, though,
that my wishes,
and my thoughts,
and my words,
don't make bad things happen.

It helps to know that every single person in the world is
sometimes sad,
sometimes scared,
sometimes angry
and worried now and then.

I know now that I can say, "I'm sorry," when I say mean things.

I know I can do some things that help me feel better.

I'm okay.

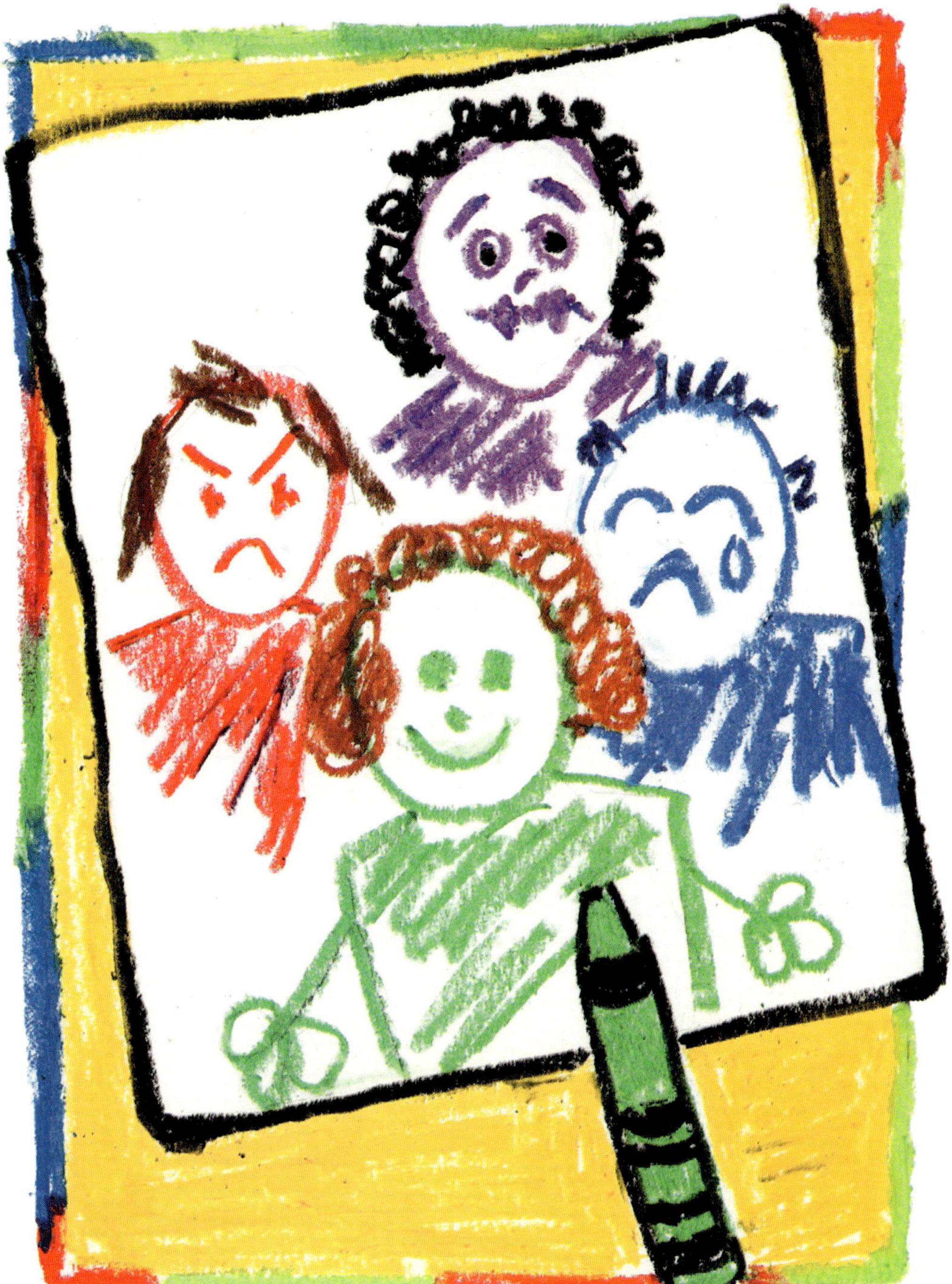

HELPING THE CHILDREN WHO KNOW THEY MADE IT HAPPEN

It seems that as parents, we spend a lot of time trying to get children to accept responsibility for the little things that they did do. Simple things like, "Who left the cereal bowl on the table? Who knocked over the flower pot?" or "Who got out the building blocks?" are often greeted by a chorus of, "Not Me!" Since children are so adept at denying responsibility, it often comes as a surprise to learn what responsibility they do take and keep to themselves.

When is my child likely to believe she made it happen? Made-it-happen thoughts occur when important life events happen. Death, divorce, injury and illness raise questions for children about security. They become aware that something could happen to other people they need and love. They also become concerned about their own safety, about something happening to them.

Why does my child believe he made it happen? Made-it-happen thoughts are often the attempt to find a cause for important events. Through believing his thoughts or actions were the cause, the child gains a sense of control over the event. If he is careful, he can make sure that the bad thing never happens again. However, such power is a tremendous responsibility and a tremendous burden. It leaves no room for mistakes, or for being human.

Made-it-happen thoughts also occur when the child has done or thought something he feels was "wrong." The thought or action may have happened minutes, hours or days before the event. Responsibility-taking springs from guilt, with the event seen as punishment. Rather than relieving guilt, the child's guilt grows. Now, she not only feels bad about what she did, but also about what happened as a result.

How can I let them know they didn't make it happen? When important events occur, talk to your child about their real causes. Children love facts, presented in simple terms. Complex situations can be simplified.

"Mommy and Daddy
are never happy together."
"Germs cause illness."
"Tiny cells that got mixed up cause cancer."
"Accidents happen when
something is out-of-control (a falling rock)
or when someone makes a mistake
(turning down a 1-way street)."

Help your child feel safe. When divorce happens, reassure him that parents never stop loving their children. When sickness occurs, talk about all the things that you and he do to keep healthy. When death occurs, let him know that the sad feelings he has will get better.

Help your child understand the limits of her power. Point out other wishes that did not come true, other times when nothing happened after angry words are spoken.

Turn guilt and regret into actions. Find things for the child to do now to deal with her feelings now.

Talk about you own feelings. As adults, our "I know I made it happen" thinking takes the form of, "I should have...If only..." As we find a way to let go of this guilt, we also gain the insight to help our children.

Remember that I-made-it-happen thoughts can be hidden for years. Keep listening to what your child says now, for it may provide secrets to old burdens as well as new ones.